THE

REVIVAL OF POPERY:

A SERMON

PREACHED BEFORE

THE UNIVERSITY OF OXFORD,

AT ST. MARY'S,

ON SUNDAY, MAY 20, 1838.

———◆———

BY

GODFREY FAUSSETT, D.D.

OF MAGDALEN COLLEGE,

THE LADY MARGARET'S PROFESSOR OF DIVINITY.

———◆———

SECOND EDITION.

———◆———

OXFORD,

AT THE UNIVERSITY PRESS, FOR THE AUTHOR.

SOLD BY JOHN HENRY PARKER:

AND BY J. G. AND F. RIVINGTON, ST. PAUL'S CHURCHYARD

AND WATERLOO-PLACE, LONDON.

1838.

THE JUNIOR STUDENTS

OF

THE UNIVERSITY OF OXFORD,

THIS SERMON

IS INSCRIBED

BY THEIR FAITHFUL FRIEND,

THE AUTHOR.

PREFACE TO SECOND EDITION.

SOME strictures on my sermon having appeared in a letter from the Rev. J. H. Newman, a brief reference to them may be required on my part. Brief however it ought to be, inasmuch as the letter is any thing but a regular answer to the sermon, and should seem to have been written without any complete perusal of it, including of course the Notes and Appendix. Hence, I presume, it is, that I am supposed to make assertions without proof (p. 6.),—and am presented with a long list of *exemplary* divines, who observed the Christian practice of *occasional fasting* and *humiliation*, in obedience to the rules of the Church, (p. 93.) as the principal answer (for mere etymology does not prove that St. Paul *bruised* his body, p. 92.) to what I had said of the gloomy views *of sin after baptism*, and of those *rigid mortifications* and *painful penances*, that *abasement of mind and body* and *utter renunciation of the world* which are suggested *to the sinner* as the *means* of *blotting out eternal torment by temporal affliction*. (Sermon, p. 17. and Appendix.)

Some oversight of the same kind, I suppose, has led Mr. Newman to complain of the application (p. 5.) of the terms "combination" and "conspiracy" to Mr. Froude and his friends, though the expressions in my pages (pp. 13. and 52.) are closely connected with their justification. Mr. Froude himself was not so nice;—he candidly avowed himself " an *ecclesiastical agitator ;*"—and expressed his fear that his correspondent and others " were going to back out of the *conspiracy*." (Remains, vol. I. pp. 258. and 377.)

Equally hasty, and still more unfortunate, is the attempt at direct contradiction to my statement, that the term *altar*, as synonymous with the *Lord's table*, does not appear to have been adopted till about the end of the second century. With an air of somewhat unseemly triumph, four passages from Ignatius are brought forward, of which however *not one* goes to the extent of proving that by the term *altar* (θυσιαστήριον) is meant the *material table* at which the communicants partook of the Eucharist;—and two *at least*, have no more reference even to a *material altar*, than the ordinary phrase " within the pale of the Church" has to a *material fence*. (p. 40.) However, not merely to assert my own judgment in opposition to Mr. Newman's, I subjoin in a note that of Abp. Usher[a]. The references to Scripture (Matt. v. 23. and Heb. xiii. 10.) are as little to the purpose; the word in the first passage meaning the *Jewish* altar; in the other, *figuratively*, the great atonement. (Vide Schleusner in voc. θυσιαστήριον.) (p. 42.) The enumeration of a dozen Fathers from near the end of the *second* to the end of the *fourth* Century, who called the *Lord's Table* the *altar*, proves no more than was already acknowledged. In fact nothing could be

a Πάντες ὡς εἷς, εἰς τὸν ναὸν Θεοῦ συντρέχετε, ὡς ἐπὶ ἓν θυσιαστήριον.] Anglican. *Omnes ut in unum templum concurrite Dei, ut in unum altare.* Ubi observa, ναὸν καὶ θυσιαστήριον *rem unam et eandem* denotare. Unde in Polycarpi ad Philippenses, et Ignatio ad Tarsenses tributâ Epistolâ, θυσιαστήριον Θεοῦ, a vulgato Latino Interprete *sacrarium Dei* recte est redditum. *Usser. in Ignatii Epist. ad Magnes. §. 7. Cotelerii Patres Apostolici, vol. II. p. 56. Edit. Amstelæd. 1724.*

Ita supra in Epistolâ ad Ephesios idem: Ἐὰν μή τις ἐντὸς ᾖ τοῦ θυσιαστηρίου, ὑστερεῖται τοῦ ἄρτου τοῦ Θεοῦ. *Nisi quis intra altare sit, privatur pane Dei:* hoc est, *intra sacrarium,* de quo vide supra in Epist. ad Magnesianos, vel *intra cœtum fidelium,* de quo Clemens Alexandrinus, lib. 7. Stromatum: Ἐστὶ γοῦν τὸ παρ' ἡμῖν θυσιαστήριον ἐνταῦθα τὸ ἐπίγειον, τὸ ἄθροισμα τῶν ταῖς εὐχαῖς ἀνακειμένων, μίαν ὥσπερ ἔχον φωνὴν τὴν κοινὴν, καὶ μίαν γνώμην. *Est igitur altare illud quod apud nos hic est in terris, cœtus ille eorum, qui hic precibus dicati sunt, unam quasi vocem communem habens et mentem unam. Ibid. in Epist. ad Trall. §. 7. Ibid. p. 63.*

Altare apud Patres, *mensam Dominicam* passim denotat: apud Ignatium et Polycarpum *sacrarium* quoque. Vide supr. in Epist. ad Magnesian. et ad Trall. *Ibid. in Philadelph. §. 4. Ibid. p. 76.*

more natural, than for Jewish and Gentile converts, with their old religious associations, to apply the term *altar*, though in *no strict* or *proper* sense, to that which they found under their adopted profession to bear the nearest analogy to it.—Just in the same way the term *altar*, though *excluded* from our formularies at the Reformation, has survived in the language of the people, and may innocently continue to do so, unless injudicious men revive the idea of its connexion with a *proper sacrifice*.

Mr. Newman appears to misapprehend my remarks on the Crucifix. Indeed he has completely mystified my language by wresting the word " *reverence*" from its *mean* position between " *worship*" and " *religious interest*," and translating it as simple *respect*.—I, on the other hand, am at a loss to understand what idea he attaches to that " *use* of the Crucifix" which he admits to prevail to a certain extent ;—what " *emblem* or *symbol*," he would insinuate, that we *may* " bow down to," as God's appointment ; and as the worship of images, which " God has " not appointed," is confessed to be idolatrous, in what cases, or " *given individuals*," it could possibly cease to be so. (p. 25.)

I shrink from characterizing the feeling, or the want of it, which can exult in the offensive display of the extravagancies of Sectarian interpretation of Prophecy against our (and Mr. Newman's ?) venerated Church, as a fair set-off against the Protestant view of its application to the Church of Rome. (p. 31—37.) However, lest any one should take fright at the tremendous alternative of our " *coming from the synagogue of Satan*," and having " *the Devil's orders*," I simply urge, in the words of an ingenious writer, " That the succession of Church offices " is no more affected by the errors of Popery, than a man's " pedigree is affected by his bodily distemper, or the dis-

" tempers of his parents ;—and if the man, by alteratives
" and restoratives, is cured with the blessing of God, he
" returns to the state of his purer ancestors of a remote
" generation [b]."

His infelicity in referring to Scripture in support of
an argument of his own on this subject, goes a step beyond that already noticed in his reference to Ignatius.
His argument in short depends, I will not say for its
soundness, but for its bare pretence to plausibility, entirely on the supposition of the *word Rome* being *literally*
found in the Apocalypse, whereas *it is not there at all !*
(p. 38.)—I would observe, however, that this avowal of
his opinion on the prophecies relating to the great Apostasy, completely bears out my inference, (Sermon, p. 26.)
that the decided advocacy of the Church of Rome, which
some persons now adopt, is quite inconsistent with their
having identified her with the mysterious " Babylon ;"—
that consequently, if our best interpreters of Prophecy be
not wholly mistaken in their views, (and, in main points
at least, I confess that I see not how they are to be con-
futed,) these persons are doing their best to blind the eyes
of thoughtless people, and at a most inauspicious period,
to a danger of awful magnitude. If the future fulfilment of Prophecy be, *in its detail*, confessedly beyond our
penetration, it is but the more imperatively required of
us " not to be high-minded, but fear," lest haply, when
the day of destruction cometh, " London" herself, (ac-
cording to Mr. Newman's flippant suggestion,) " with
" her ships and sailors, merchants and merchandise," be
actually found within the devoted precinct.

The determination to maintain the comparative inno-
cence of Popery *before the Council of Trent*, is even more
decisively evinced in Mr. Newman's letter, than in the

[b] " Short View," &c. Scholar Armed, vol. II. p. 57.

instances to which I have already adverted. While the force of plain historical truth compels the confession, that Image-worship was sanctioned at the second Council of Nicæa, (why not add A. D. 787?) and Transubstantiation at the Fourth Lateran, (why not add A. D. 1215?), and that other abuses (no date given) preceded the Council of Trent, it is declared of these notorious and inveterate corruptions that they were for the most part " *in* the Church, but not *of* it ;"—*floating* opinions " and practices," (p. 13.)—"doctrines *doubtfully* broached " or *factiously* defended;" " the *private* and unresolved " opinions of *some certain only*;" (p. 15, 16.)—and that " if Rome has apostatized, it was at the time of the " Council of Trent." (p. 14.)—On the other hand, a sort of merit is made, of one of the " Tracts for the " Times" having declared in large letters, to draw attention, that " while Rome *is what it is*, union with it is " impossible;" (p. 18.)—and of Mr. Froude's calling the Council of Trent " atrocious," and " wishing for the " total overthrow of the system, which is built upon it." (p. 12.)—But who, let me ask, is to be deceived by all this? and where lies the doubt, as to the wished-for inference with regard to Rome, *as she was* before the Reformation? Let Mr. Froude, who is happily somewhat more given to plainness of speech than his abettors, be permitted to speak out for himself and them, and tell us *why* he hated the Council of Trent, and Rome *as she is*. " I shall not," says he, " ever abuse the Roman " Catholics, as a Church, *for any thing except excommuni-* " *cating us*." (Remains, p. 395.) " ——— admits, that if " the Roman Catholics would *revoke their anathemas*, we " might reckon all the points of difference as *theological* " *opinions*. This τόπος is a good one." (*Ibid.* p. 320.)

Mr. Newman asks, (p. 42.) " In what sense do you " mean that the *writers* of the Tracts appeal to the

" *Lutherans*, when *not* the writers, but *only Bp. Cosin* in
" the Tracts, appeals, *not* to the Lutherans, but the
" *whole Protestant world?*"—This is utterly uncandid,
and must not be allowed to pass.—The Tract, No. 27,
is a Treatise of Bp. Cosin's; but being *adopted as a
Tract*, becomes from that moment, *every letter of it*, the
avowed language of the *Tract writers*. They *do appeal
distinctly* to the *Lutherans* (the known supporters of *Consubstantiation*) and *to the whole Protestant world*, at a period,
unluckily, when a belief in the *real presence*, closely bor-
dering on *Consubstantiation*, was widely prevalent. (See
Note C. Appendix.) England notoriously presented no
exception to this, in the age of Laud and Cosin, (the
pattern age of Mr. Froude and the Tract writers.)
Cosin cites Bilson and Andrews, as arguing thus with
the Papists. " Christ said, ' *This is my body;*' in this,
" the object, we *are agreed* with you; the *manner* only
" is controverted. We hold by a firm belief, that *it is
" the body* of Christ ;—of the *manner* how it comes to be
" so, there is not a word in the Gospel." (Tract 27.
p. 4.)—Bramhall, as cited by Mr. Newman, (p. 20.) says,
" Abate us *Transubstantiation*, and those things which
" are consequent of their determination of the *manner*
" of presence, and we have *no difference* with them (the
" Romanists) in this particular."

A reluctant admission that Mr. Froude allowed, in
some sort, a *local* presence of Christ's human nature in
the elements, (p. 51.) is followed by a singular attempt
(p. 53–63.) to *shew*, by a subtle distinction, that Christ's
body may be *locally* in heaven, yet at the same time *really*,
though not *locally*, here. " But it is idle," says Professor
Hey, " to use words, and by limitations to take away
" their customary meaning. As words are arbitrary
" signs, they depend for their meaning on custom wholly.
" What signifies talking of *a body* not present as *to place?*

" That which is not present in such a sense as to occupy " a place, is not *body*, in human language [c]." Our congregations must be treated as people of plain understandings. If Mr. Newman addresses *his* with subtleties of the kind now adverted to, they will either believe in *both the real and the local* presence ; or, remembering the caution of our Church, that " the natural body and blood " of our Saviour Christ are in heaven, and not here ; it " being against the truth of Christ's natural body to be " at once in more places than one [d] ;" they will believe *neither the one nor the other*. In the first case, as to a most important article of their faith, they will *become Papists ;* in the other, they will inevitably *take him for a Papist*, and respect his ministrations accordingly. In the mean time, what becomes of the creed of the Pastor himself? The much vaunted " via media" is after all but a treacherous and slippery path, and it is clear enough on which side lies the declivity.

An ambiguous phrase or two in the Formularies or Homilies of our Church, such as, " verily and indeed " taken and received,"—" no untrue figure of a thing " absent," &c. (p. 46.) depending entirely for their meaning on the idea attached to the *real presence*, and decisively explained by her more cautious language elsewhere adopted, such as that just now referred to, afford *no decent pretence* for the assertion, that she countenances such views as those of Mr. Froude, or the writers of the Tracts. The " glowing thoughts," and eloquent expressions of Hooker, *judiciously* qualified as they are, by his " *causes instrumental*,"—" *as touching efficacy, force, and* " *virtue*,".&c. will not bear them out (p. 67.) ; and if they did, be it remembered, we do not *swear by* Hooker, any more than we do by the *rhetorical figures* of Chrysostom,

c Hey's Divinity Lectures, vol. iv. p. 352.
d Protestation at the end of the Communion Service.

(p. 80.) or the *superstitious credulity* of Cyprian, (p. 78.) whose belief in the miraculous sickness of the child at the sacrament is as little calculated to do credit to his judgment, as the avowed adoption of it is to raise the reputation of Mr. Newman.

With reference to the profane Corinthians, it is argued that " the phrases ' eating and drinking judgment unto " himself, as not discerning the Lord's body,' and ' being " guilty of the body and blood of the Lord,' certainly do " seem to imply some special act of blasphemy, of which " the doctrine of *the real presence does*, and the doctrine " of mere appropriation *does not* supply a sufficient ex- " planation." (p. 83.) Now, not to waste time on an argument from which piety at once recoils, it is a singular fact, and the coincidence is most instructive, that this is the identical argument of the *avowed Papist* Dr. Wiseman, who remarks that " St. Paul characterises " the transgression, just as he would transgressions " against the *real body* of Christ *if present*, but in words " totally inapplicable to the Eucharist, if these be absent " from it e." I would not insinuate that Mr. Newman has actually borrowed his weapon from the armoury of the enemy, but merely that having both of them, in every practical view, the same cause to defend, they have with instinctive sympathy caught up the same sophistry. It is a mere delusion to imagine that the denial of *transubstantiation* is the denial of the *Popish doctrine*. The *gross fable* has long since found more or less of a *spiritual* interpretation among the more intelligent of the Papists themselves ;—but a belief in a *real presence* still remains, which quite as effectually *deifies* the elements, and sustains the *idolatries* of the *mass*.

After all, however, the prominent feature of Mr. New-

e Wiseman's Lectures on the **Real Presence**, &c. p. **266.**

man's Letter is its constant appeal, page after page, to a confused and wearisome medley of *human* and *traditional* authority, coupled with the comparative neglect of that *unerring rule* which can alone decide the points at issue. It seems the inveterate habit of his mind, imparting a tone and colour to his ordinary phraseology, even where no direct appeal is thought of. Thus we are recommended to " throw ourselves into that system of " truth, which our fathers have handed down even " through the worst of times ;" (p. 98.)—we are reminded of " the pleasant and fair pastures of Catholic " doctrine, which are our heritage ;" (p. 71.)—of " the " spirit, the truth, the old Catholic life and power which " is in" certain opinions; (p. 4.)—and we are exhorted to " live up to the *creeds*, the *services*, the *ordinances*, the " *usages* of our own *Church* ;" (p. 98.)—but why not up to the *precepts of the Gospel* also ?

Much in the same spirit, and under what influence no one doubts, the *British Critic*, referring to my Sermon, says, that " at this time of day the word of no one man, " unsupported by argument or appeal to authority, can " stop the course of thought in the University, or deter " inquiring minds from *following the paths of Hooker, Andrews, and Bull, or of their masters Irenæus or Cyprian*[f]." But what, it may be asked, " stopped the course of" the sentence, in its natural ascent to the *masters of these masters, the inspired Apostles and Evangelists of Jesus Christ ?*

Oxford, July 13, 1838.

[f] British Critic for July, 1838, p. 232.

REVELATION xviii. 4.

*Come out of her, my people, that ye be not par-
takers of her sin, and that ye receive not of her
plagues.*

TO the sincere and reflecting members of our
Reformed and Apostolical Church, grateful
for her emancipation from the spiritual thral-
dom and degrading superstitions of former
centuries, and cherishing the hope of her pre-
serving, through the Divine blessing, the pure
light of Gospel truth to the end of time, few
subjects can appear more calculated to awaken,
if not absolute and immediate alarm, yet at
least anxious thought and gloomy forebodings,
than the rapid revival of the tenets and the
influence of Romanism, which it is our lot to
witness. Neither can it be supposed to allay
their apprehensions, still less to afford them
consolation, to be convinced, as they can
scarcely fail to be, that the unwonted impulse,
which has been given to this insidious and
encroaching system, is the result of our own
preposterous impolicy.

Experience, the never-failing and effectual
guide of individual conduct, seems to be lost
to the observation of communities. In spite
of all the lessons of history, occupying, as it
may be said to do, the place of national ex-

perience, men appear still prone to pursue in their collective capacity the same blind course of folly and improvidence and failure, ultimately and providentially leading, through discipline and affliction, to repentance and recovery ; and, allowing for a few minor modifications arising from times and circumstances, to be carried on in a perpetually revolving circle of causes and consequences to the same inevitable results. The recorded conflicts and sufferings and deliverances of our Church and nation, have faded from the memory of succeeding generations, leaving the impression rather of fable than of fact. The Popery of the present day is no longer regarded as the same Popery which kindled the fires of the Marian persecution, revelled in the tortures of the Inquisition, and overspread the face of Europe with devastation and massacre ;—or if it be admitted that her principles are notoriously unchanged, and avowedly unchangable, the guarantee of increasing intelligence and civilization on the one hand, and of the decline of the temporal power of Rome on the other, is confidently appealed to as ample security against every recurrence of barbarous atrocity ; and political power is once more rashly committed to those hands, which, to say the least, never employed it, and can never be expected to employ it, but to persecute and oppress the advocates of a purer faith.

Moreover, as though our own power were far above the danger of assault, and our own religious principles beyond the reach of perversion or alloy—and we regarded with equal contempt the superstition and the dominion of Rome—every facility for the dissemination of her tenets is allowed to exist among us. In the plenitude of our infatuated liberality we connive at the revival of monastic establishments; and even those societies, which are so notoriously objectionable as to find no rest for the sole of their foot in a neighbouring country, though professing allegiance to the Papal See, obtain a sure refuge in this common and undisturbed receptacle of all that is religious or irreligious—all that worships God in truth or in heresy — all that forgets or denies him [a]. And the consequences are such as it required no prophet to foretell. In an important portion of our empire Popery once more rears her mitred head; re-assumes, in defiance of violated law, her dignities and titles of honour, re-erects the Cathedral and the Palace, and anticipates—and who shall say without some grounds for such anticipation?—the early prostration of the Protestant esta-

[a] It appears that there are now in England no less than eighteen nunneries, and that a society of Trappists (who are understood to have been refused a settlement in Normandy) are established near Ashby-de-la-Zouche. *L'Ami de la Religion, Journal Ecclésiastique; Paris, Mardi, 9 Mai,* 1837.

blishment under her own restored supremacy [b]. In our own land, too, her seminaries and places of [c] worship have been rapidly multiplying around us, and the tide of Papal superstition, which at its lowest ebb was overlooked as insignificant, and in a measure forgotten, is so obviously rising on us, that men of seriousness and reflection are already, " musing in their hearts" what chastisements may yet be in store for this Church and nation, the meet reward of an ungrateful insensibility to past deliverances and present blessings.

One thing at least is certain, that a revival of the contest between the Churches of England and of Rome has become inevitable, or rather that it has actually commenced; and that, inasmuch as it has fallen on us almost by surprise, it has found us very imperfectly pre-

[b] " It is some consolation to reflect that the legislative axe " is laid to the root of the Establishment. The pruners of " the Ecclesiastical vineyard have not read the Roman history " in vain, and already ten of the lofty plants, which poisoned " by their narcotic influence the wholesome vegetation, are " laid low. This, doubtless, is a prelude to a further and " more enlarged process of expurgation. With every successive " measure of reform, existing abuses will be removed, until, it " is to be hoped, not a vestige of the mighty nuisance will " remain." *Letter from Dr. M'Hale to the Bishop of Exeter.—Times, August* 9, 1833.

[c] There are now 430 Roman Catholic chapels in England. That of Moor Fields, which at the beginning of the century had within its district a population of 5000 or 6000 Roman Catholics, has now 30,000. *L'Ami de la Religion, Journal Ecclesiastique; Paris, Mardi,* 9 *Mai,* 1837.

pared for our defence;—it has overtaken us when labouring under the weakness consequent on almost unexampled disunion, both civil and religious; a disadvantage of the most formidable character, when our adversaries are at once subtle and insidious in policy, and united in purpose.

It is not however my object to invite your attention either to that large and respectable class of persons, who, with an unaffected though misguided liberality of feeling, committed the grievous error of mistaking a religious question for one of a simply political nature; or to that, it is to be feared, still more numerous band of the profane and licentious, the indifferent and sceptical, who could not but regard with utter contempt the principles to which I am adverting. A sad experience is rapidly curing the one, and the other are, for the most part, hopelessly inaccessible to religious considerations. But it deeply concerns us to direct our serious thoughts to the condition of the really religious sections of our community, to their views and principles, and to the false and unfavourable position occupied by some among them with reference to the impending struggle.

Now there are notoriously existing among us a large and influential body of Christians, consisting, chiefly, of the dissenting Sects, which fell into schism at or near the period of the Reformation; of those other denominations which have more recently seceded from the Church; and, unhappily we may add, of those also, who, though nominally members of the Church of England, have in some measure adopted Sectarian views. All these persons, however widely they may differ from each other on many points, naturally constitute but one class, as far as concerns the matter now before us; viz. that of those who despise or lightly regard Ecclesiastical Authority and Christian Unity, the claims of an Apostolical Episcopacy, the Divine commission of the Christian Priesthood; who neglect the guidance of their appointed Pastors, put no faith in their exclusive importance as the Ministers and Stewards of God's holy mysteries, and, by a chain of consequences as necessary as it is deplorable, degrade the Sacraments themselves to a corresponding level; either regarding them merely as initiatory and commemorative rites, or, at the best, losing more or less of their implicit reliance on them as the seals of the Christian Covenant—the efficacious means of grace and salvation. On the other hand, while they thus undervalue the authority and importance of the Church, they as proudly exalt their own, claiming the unlimited exercise of private judgment in the interpretation of Scripture, and maintaining the undoubted capacity for such judgment in all ordinary Christians.

With what prospect of success, it may well

be asked, could the advocate of such views as these enter the lists of controversy with the subtle Romanist? Amid all the errors and corruptions of Popery, enormous as they are, she has not absolutely failed to retain a portion of truth ; and this truth, abused though it be in her hands to the purposes of sacerdotal influence, and disguised and distorted by superstition, is precisely that which, when skilfully displayed, is calculated to put to shame and confusion the impugners of Ecclesiastical authority, the despisers of the Ministerial functions, and the desecrators of the Sacraments. In fact, the arrogant claims to independent judgment in religious matters, however vaunted in theory, are ever repudiated by the general practice of mankind, and are utterly inconsistent with the wants and weaknesses of our common nature. The great bulk of every community notoriously consists of those who, from youth, or defective education, or weakness of judgment, or engrossing avocations, or other causes which need no farther enumeration, are utterly incapacitated for originating and completing their religious inquiries for themselves. Authority of some description or other is their sole dependence:—in matters of such high interest as the awful alternatives of a future state, they cannot rest till they have reposed their confidence somewhere. And if the legitimate claim to their religious trust be coldly withheld, or, at the most, indecisively proposed to them, their most natural refuge is in the bosom of that which assumes to itself the character of an Infallible Church.

The folly and the danger of the latitudinarian and schismatical irregularities thus unhappily characteristic of our Church and Country, have been from time to time powerfully exposed by the zeal and learning of her members, and sounder views of Christian Unity, Ecclesiastical Subordination, the Ministerial Office, the Sacramental Ordinances, and other strictly Catholic principles, have been in some degree rescued from the almost general neglect and obloquy to which the spirit of a thoughtless and licentious age had consigned them. And still more recently it has fallen to our lot to witness—and God grant, that not-withstanding present untoward appearances, we may even yet deem it our happiness and privilege to have witnessed—a combination of talent and learning and industry, directed to the same important objects with a zeal and devotedness worthy of the purest ages of Christianity. It has become, however, no longer possible to disguise the painful fact, that the hopes thus excited have been succeeded by at least a temporary disappointment, and by a feeling of suspicion and even alarm, which the most candid and dispassionate observers no longer pronounce to be either vague or indefinite or unfounded ; that the zealous efforts to revive a due respect for Ecclesiastical and properly Catholic princi- ples, have been far too little connected with the requisite caution regarding their inveterate abuse by the Church of Rome; and that amidst much of important truth elicited and displayed, an alloy of Popish error and super- stition has undeniably insinuated itself[c].

The general object being at once so de- sirable and so ably pursued, a few unguarded statements, the result probably of individual haste and indiscretion—and it might have been hoped, abandoned on reflection by the authors themselves—it would have been pre- mature, it might even have been injudicious, to notice with any severity of censure. But when they assume more and more unequivo- cally the marks of deliberation and design, the evidence of numbers and of combination; when the most plausible palliations of Ro- mish corruption, and the most insidious cavils against the wisdom, and even in some mea- sure the necessity, of the Reformation, find their way into the periodical and popular and most widely disseminated literature of the day;—when the wild and visionary sentiments of an enthusiastic mind, involving in their

[c] This has at length become so notorious, that the Roman- ists themselves, not in this country only, but on the conti- nent, are deriving hope and encouragement from our pre- sumed change of views and principles. See Appendix, note A.

unguarded expression an undisguised prefer-
ence for a portion at least of Papal superstition, and occasionally even a wanton outrage
on the cherished feelings of the sincere Protestant—his pious affection for those venerated
names which he habitually associates with the
inestimable blessings of the Reformation[d]—
are dragged forth from the sanctuary of con-
fidential intercourse, and recommended to the
public as " a witness of Catholic views," and
to " speak a word in season for the Church of
" God[e];" as " likely to suggest thoughts on
" doctrine, on Church policy, and on indivi-
" dual conduct, most true and most necessary

[d] " As to the Reformers, I think worse and worse of them.
" Jewell was what you would in these days call an irreve-
" rent dissenter. His Defence of his Apology disgusted me
" more than almost any work I have read." *Remains of the
late Rev. Richard Hurrell Froude, M.A. Fellow of Oriel College*, vol. I. p. 380.

Also, " Why do you praise Ridley? Do you know suffi-
" cient good about him to counterbalance the fact, that he
" was the associate of Cranmer, Peter Martyr, and Bucer?
" N. B. How beautifully the Edinburgh Review has shewn
" up Luther, Melancthon, and Co.! What good genius has
" possessed them to do our dirty work?......*Pour moi*, I never
" mean, if I can help it, to use any phrases even, which can
" connect me with such a set. I shall never call the Holy
" Eucharist ' the Lord's Supper,' nor God's Priests, ' Min-
" isters of the Word,' nor the Altar, ' the Lord's Table,' &c.
" &c.;—innocent as such phrases are in themselves, they
" have been dirtied; a fact of which you seem oblivious on
" many occasions." *Ibid.* p. 394, 395.

[e] Preface to Froude's Remains, p. xxii.

" for. these times," and as " a bold and com-
" prehensive sketch of a new position" for the
Church of England [f];—and this too under circumstances which imply the concurrence and
approval, and responsibility too, of an indefinite and apparently numerous body of friends
and correspondents and editors and reviewers ;
—who shall any longer deny the imperative necessity which exists for the most decisive language of warning and caution, lest these rash
projectors of " a new position" for our Church
should be unwarily permitted to undermine
and impair her old and approved defences?

The leading particulars in which this increasing aberration from Protestant principles
has displayed itself, may perhaps be considered as the following :—a disposition to over-
rate the importance of Apostolical Tradition,
and the authoritative teaching of the Church ;
—exaggerated and unscriptural statements of
doctrine with regard to the two Sacraments ;
—and a general tendency on the one hand to
depreciate the principles of Protestantism and
the character and conduct of the Reformers,
and on the other, not indeed absolutely to
deny the grosser corruptions of Popery, but
so far to palliate her errors, and display in the
most favourable light whatever remnant of
good she still retains, as to leave it in a man-

[f] British Critic for January 1838, p. 225.

ner doubtful to which side the balance of truth inclines, and to banish from the mind of the unwary Protestant every idea of the extreme guilt and danger of a reunion with an Idolatrous and Antichristian Apostasy.

With regard to the Traditions of the Church, as an authority distinct from Holy Scripture, independently of the vast extent of the subject, there are obvious and special reasons why I must on this day g decline to enter on their consideration. Suffice it to say, that within due limits, and on certain subjects, and in legitimate subordination to inspired truth, the principle is not merely useful, but necessary, being dangerous only by excess or abuse, or when not scrupulously disengaged from those polluted channels, in exploring which, extreme distrust is natural, and extreme caution indispensable.

The discussion of Baptismal Regeneration also would carry us far beyond the limits of the present opportunity; not to mention that the gloomy views of sin after Baptism, now professed by some persons, which have chiefly called forth animadversion and complaint, are no direct revival of Popish error, though it must be admitted that they have unhappily found a natural and easy connection with those rigid mortifications, and

g The day on which one of the Bampton Lecture Sermons on the same subject was also preached.

self-abasements, and painful penances [h], which call us back at once to the darkest period of Roman superstition; and which have an evident tendency hopelessly to alarm and repel those abettors of low and rationalistic views of the Sacramental Ordinances, whom it is our especial object to win and persuade to a saving faith in their genuine and inestimable importance.

The Sacrament of the Lord's Supper, however, both with reference to the superstitions notoriously engrafted on it by the Church of Rome, and the gradual and near approximation towards the same superstitions recently observable in the views of some members of our own Communion, requires a more distinct and particular consideration. Of all the peculiar tenets of Romanism, none probably can, to common apprehension, appear less reconcilable to reason or Scripture, or more worthy of those ages of intellectual darkness during which it acquired its ascendancy, than that of Transubstantiation. It is probably as difficult for my present hearers to understand our Saviour literally, when he said, " This is " my body," " This is my blood," as when, on other occasions, he described himself as " the door of the sheep [i]," or " the true vine [k]." It is equally incredible, or rather absolutely

[h] See Appendix, Note B.   [i] John x. 7.   [k] John xv. 1.

impossible, that the Apostles should have imagined that the very same body, in which, in its full integrity, their blessed Master stood visibly before them, was also in his hands, and offered to them to be eaten. We know in fact, that they had no idea of such a marvellous transformation ; that they considered, that when Christians " ate of that bread and " drank of that cup, they shewed" (καταγγέλλετε, *ye declare* or *commemorate*) " the Lord's " death[1]," representing by visible symbols his absent body and blood : and moreover, that when, in obedience to his commands, they " did this in remembrance of him," " the cup " of blessing which they blessed, and the " bread which they brake," were effectually made to them " the *communion*" (κοινωνία, *communication, participation*) " of his body and " blood[m]," of the benefits of his sufferings and death.

The case of the profane Corinthians[n] is a sufficient proof that they had never heard of Transubstantiation. Had St. Paul inculcated upon them that doctrine, or any other modification of the *real presence* of Christ's body and blood in the elements of bread and wine, their conduct would have been not simply incredible, but morally impossible. It is no less evident that they ate at a *table*, not at an *altar*.

[1] 1 Cor. xi. 26.   [m] 1 Cor. x. 16.   [n] 1 Cor. xi.

Indeed the term *altar*, as synonymous with the Lord's table, does not appear to have been adopted till about the end of the second century; and then merely in a figurative sense, and out of a spirit of accommodation, as it should seem, and with a view to conciliate the prejudices of Jews and Pagans, who habitually reproached the Christians as having neither altar nor sacrifice[o]. The early Fathers constantly designate the bread and wine as " signs," " symbols," " figures," " sacraments," —not indeed as empty signs, but as attended by the blessing of Christ who instituted them, and as efficacious to the worthy receiver.

It would be tedious, as it is unnecessary, to trace the progressive encroachments of Superstition to its final triumph over plain Scripture and right reason. The gross idea of the corporal presence in the Sacrament was not of very early growth in the Christian Church. Its origin is generally assigned to the eighth century, and its decided adoption by the Church of Rome to the eleventh[p]:—but from that moment she became fully sensible of its

[o] Justin Martyr, Apol. 2. Origen, contra Cels. lib. 8.

[p] Berenger's recantation of his opposition to this doctrine was forced on him by pope Nicholas II. and the Roman Council A. D. 1058. *Mosheim, Eccl. Hist.* vol. II. p. 561. It was finally established by Innocent III, and the 4th Lateran Council A. D. 1215. *Ibid.* vol. III. p. 243.

paramount importance to her views and interests. Investing the priesthood with a character almost superhuman, and with an influence proportionably unbounded over an ignorant and credulous age, it became the corner-stone of that spiritual despotism which she erected upon the liberties and consciences of mankind : and, strange as this may now appear to those whose minds have never been subjected to the overwhelming prejudice, it was, of all the superstitions of Romanism, the one from which the Reformers found the greatest difficulty in emancipating themselves. The actual worship, the absolute deification of the Sacramental elements which the Church of Rome maintained, had habituated pious and humble minds to such a devout reverence for them, that they could not approach the consideration of the sacred subject of the Eucharist without such impressions of awe as necessarily disturbed the calm exercise of their reasoning powers. It is notorious, that Cranmer himself had been for many years engaged in forwarding the English Reformation before he could succeed in reforming his own convictions on this point. Luther indeed, and many other of the German reformers, may fairly be considered never to have fully escaped from the inveterate prejudice. In specious opposition indeed to Popery, they took refuge in what has been termed Consubstantiation, thereby adopting a distinction without any practical difference. For if, in denying the gross, organic, and tangible change, a *real* and *substantial* presence of the body and blood of Christ be still admitted to be combined *with* the bread and wine—if the subtle refinement still leaves behind and involved in the consecrated elements a *present* body and *present* Deity—it would be difficult to assign a reason, why the elevation and worship of the host, and the whole train of attendant superstition which followed the Popish version of the doctrine, may not as naturally be deduced from this also.

I have been thus particular in calling your attention to this marked feature of the early days of the Reformation, that you may the better appreciate the alarming fact, that it is to those half-converted German Reformers, and to the strong and unguarded expressions which their works supply, that appeal is now made by members of our Church, for their statements of the doctrine of the Eucharist; such as, " that the bread and wine are " not the signs of the absent body and blood " of Christ"—" that the true body and blood " of Christ are truly presented, given, and re- " ceived together with the visible signs of " bread and wine ;" " that Christ in his holy " Supper gives us the true and proper sub-

" stance of his body and blood q." Now granting that these expressions may be, and indeed are, generally qualified by assigning to them a spiritual sense—this is obviously insufficient. The Papist himself, when not too closely pressed by the decrees of his Church, is occasionally found to admit that the presence is not strictly corporal. The distinction required clearly lies between the body and blood of Christ being *spiritually included* in the elements, and *spiritually received* by the faithful; or, as Bishop Taylor explains it, " We by the real " spiritual presence of Christ do understand " Christ to be present, as the Spirit of God is " present in the hearts of the faithful, by " blessing and grace r."

The naked and unqualified and therefore ambiguous expression *real presence*, now so systematically and studiously adopted by some persons, is highly objectionable and dangerous: and there is but too much reason to apprehend that some of those who employ it are far even from intending the supposed qualification. Those at least cannot intend it who advance the startling position,

q Tracts for the Times, vol. I. No. 27. See Appendix, note C.

r Bishop Taylor of the Real and Spiritual Presence of Christ in the Holy Sacrament. Section I. See Appendix, note D.

" that the power of *making* the body and
" blood of Christ is vested in the successors of
" the Apostles [s];" who pronounce the expression " Lord's table," authorized, as it is by
Scripture and our Church, to be so polluted
by Protestant use, as to be no longer fitted
to designate the *altar*[t]; who are become so
sensitive with regard to the altar itself, as to
attach importance even to the situation of a
pulpit, lest it stand in the light of what " is
" more sacred than the Holy of Holies[u];" and
who with reference, no doubt, to the " sacri-
" fice of praise and thanksgiving," and other
well-guarded language of our Liturgy, declare
our present Communion-service to be " a
" judgment on the Church[x]," and point out
the advantage of " replacing it by a good
" translation of the liturgy of St. Peter[y]."

[s] " I should like to know why you flinch from saying that
" the power of making the body and blood of Christ is vested
" in the Successors of the Apostles." *Froude's Remains*,
vol. I. p. 326.

[t] Ibid. ut supra.

[u] " If you are determined to have a pulpit in your church,
" which I had rather be without, do put it at the west end of
" the church, or leave it where it is : every one can hear you
" perfectly, and what can they want more? But whatever
" you do, pray don't let it stand in the light of the Altar,
" which, if there is any truth in my notions of Ordination, is
" more sacred than the Holy of Holies was in the Jewish
" temple." *Ibid.* p. 372.

[x] Ibid. p. 410.   [y] Ibid. p. 387.

To affirm that these persons are strictly Papists, or that within certain limits of their own devising they are not actually opposed to the corruptions and the Communion of Rome, would, I am well aware, be as uncharitable as it is untrue. But who shall venture to pronounce them safe and consistent members of the Church of England? and who shall question the obvious tendency of their views to Popery itself? For if by some happy inconsistency they are themselves, and for the present, saved from the natural consequences of their own reasoning, what shall we hope for the people at large, should these delusive speculations (which God in his infinite mercy forbid) extend their influence beyond the circle (and it is hoped not yet a very extensive circle) of educated men, to which they are at present limited? If such should become the ordinary instruction of the unwary pastor to his credulous flock, what shall preserve them from all the fascinations and idolatries of the Mass, or from welcoming with open arms those crafty emissaries who have already succeeded to such a fearful extent in reimposing the yoke of spiritual bondage on the neck of our deluded countrymen?

In the more general tendency to depreciate the principles of the Reformation and palliate the errors of Romanism, to which I have before adverted, the most marked and striking feature is the studious attempt to draw a broad line of distinction between Popery *before* and Popery *since* the Council of Trent; to maintain that the religion of Rome, " so " far as relates to those particulars in which " it differs from our own, is in strictness a new " religion, having its origin with that ever-to- " be-lamented Council [z];" and we are told in plain terms, that " for this, Christendom has " to thank Luther and the Reformers[a]." And what is the natural and inevitable inference? —that the Reformation, which in all the blindness of Protestant prejudice we gratefully regard as the very chiefest of blessings,— as the revival of pure religion after ages of superstition and idolatry,—was for the most part unnecessary, and of course a flagrant and unjustifiable breach of Catholic communion.

[z] " We commonly but carelessly acquiesce in the notion— " fatal as, were it true, it would prove to the Catholicism " of our English Church—that the religion now taught by the " Church of Rome, was the religion once spread over Western " Europe, our own island included, and that our Protestant " doctrines are comparatively new among us. Whereas the " fact is, that the religion of existing Rome, so far as relates " to those particulars in which it differs from our own, is in " strictness a new religion, having its origin with the ever- " to-be-lamented Council of Trent." *British Critic, for July* 1836, p. 52.

[a] Froude's Remains, vol. I. p. 307. See Appendix, note E.

How far this novel view of History, and, I may add, of Prophecy too, may have made men the apologists of Popery, as though she were unjustly calumniated and defamed, or how far, on the other hand, an admiration for some of her principles may have made them desirous of casting a veil of oblivion over the rest, it is not possible precisely to determine. These views, indeed, may in all probability have exercised a reciprocal influence on each other. But we can scarcely be mistaken in assigning the larger share of the supposed influence to the latter. How indeed else can we account for the prejudice which can overlook the idolatries and superstitions of her early career, the superadded impostures and cruelties of succeeding ages, and the portentous accumulation of abuses in faith and practice, which, when finally viewed by the light of reviving intelligence, absolutely *compelled* the Reformation;—or which can fail to recognise in them the clear fulfilment of those memorable prophecies of the great Apostasy, of which few indeed, with the exception of the Papists themselves, have for centuries past denied the obvious application?

These persons at least can scarcely be supposed to have identified the mysterious "Babylon," " the mother of harlots and abominations of the " earth [b]," " the woman sitting on the seven

b Rev. xvii. 5.

" mountains[c]," " the great city which reigneth
" over the kings of the earth[d]," with idolatrous
and Papal Rome ; or to recognise in her Communion those who " give heed to doctrines of
" demons" or souls of departed men ; " forbid-
" ding to marry, and commanding to abstain
" from meats[e];"—to have discovered in St.
Paul's " Man of Sin, who opposeth and exalteth
" himself above all that is called God, or that is
" worshipped, so that he as God sitteth in the
" temple of God, shewing that he is God[f],"
the blasphemous titles and assumptions of the
supreme head of the Romish Church—or his
" signs and lying wonders with all deceivable-
" ness of unrighteousness[g]," in the shameless
impostures and lying legends, with which she
has for ages deluded her enslaved and credulous votaries. Least of all can they apprehend the awful and sudden destruction which
has been prophetically denounced against
her[h], or be giving heed to the timely warning,
" Come out of her, my people, that ye be not
" partakers of her sins, and that ye receive
" not of her plagues[i]." It is, however, at all
events, not too much to assume, that, making
due allowance for differences of opinion as to
the minute interpretation of particular points,
such is the prevailing belief of English Pro-

[c] Rev. xvii. 9.   [d] Rev. xvii. 18.   [e] 1 Tim. iv. 1, 3.
[f] 2 Thess. ii. 3, 4.   [g] 2 Thess. ii. 9, 10.   [h] Rev. xviii. 8.
[i] Rev. xviii. 4.

testants; and that, supposing even but a fair probability of its general truth, it merits the most serious consideration in times like the present[k].

But as Idolatry (spiritual fornication) is the head and front of her offences, as it is that sin for which, of all others, we have inspired authority for anticipating the severest vengeance of Heaven; and which is the most distinct characteristic of the predicted Apostasy;—as, nevertheless, the Church of Rome endeavours to evade the charge by explaining her image-worship as a merely representative and commemorative system, a few moments' attention to this point may be required. So early did the symptoms of Idolatry develope themselves in the Roman Church, that instead of a novelty, they may be in some sort regarded as the continuation, or at the least the very early revival under a new form, of the inveterate usages of Paganism. No sooner had Imperial authority declared Christianity to be the Religion of the State, than worldly views rather than sincere conversion brought numerous adherents to her Communion; and the compromising policy of the Roman Bishops led them in some measure to indulge those Heathen predilections for visible objects of worship which they could not wholly eradicate. The sacred cross—the tombs and relics

[k] See Appendix, note F.

of martyrs—the pictures and images of Apostles and Saints—gradually became objects of
religious veneration ; the veneration thus naturally excited insensibly advanced to actual
worship ; and the simplicity of primitive
piety, the reasonable and spiritual service of
the Almighty Creator and Redeemer and
Sanctifier of mankind, was superseded by the
invocation of Saints ; accompanied, no doubt,
in the vulgar mind, with as abject a homage
to their images of wood and stone as ever was
paid to the idols of Paganism.

In fact, independently of the connexion between Pagan and Popish Idolatry observable
in this particular case, it is by no means easy
to trace the moral discrimination between
them, either in their origin or in their effects.
The hero of Heathen Antiquity and the Romish Saint arrived at the honours of worship
by a process completely similar ; and the excuse of a merely commemorative intention is
quite as reasonable in the one case as in the
other. The educated Pagan was not likely
to have confounded the image with the absolute Deity any more than the Papist himself.
But who, under either system, shall limit the
tendencies of popular superstition ;—of that
tendency chiefly by which the visible image
insensibly supersedes, in the estimation of the
ordinary worshipper, the being whom it is
supposed to represent? For without some idea

of peculiar sanctity attached to an image, as such, how shall we account for the crowds of pilgrims who flock to certain favourite shrines of the Virgin or other Saints, when the presumed object of their mistaken devotion might have been worshipped without toil or expense at home?

He who " knoweth what is in man" has prohibited the " graven image," not of false gods alone, but of the one true God himself[1]; there is neither exception nor reserve even for the image of the Incarnate Word. Will it then be credited by any one not already cognizant of the fact, that the crucifix, the effective engine, the notorious emblem of Romish superstition, is once more becoming, with some professed Protestants, an object, not indeed of worship—scarcely let us hope even of reverence—yet at least of religious interest. "The " beginning," as " of strife," so of every other evil, " is as when one letteth out water[m]." It is an experiment full of fearful hazard, yea rather of awful presumption. Pride, the primeval curse of man's race, still pursues him. God issues a prohibition; man comprehends

[1] " Take ye therefore good heed unto yourselves; for ye " saw no manner of similitude on the day that the Lord " spake unto you in Horeb out of the midst of the fire: lest " ye corrupt yourselves, and make you a graven image, the " similitude of any figure, the likeness of male or female." *Deut.* iv. 15, 16.

[m] Prov. xvii. 1.

not its reason or its purpose; he longs for clearer apprehensions of things unseen; it is a thing " to be desired to make one wise [n]." Vain man would be wiser than his God.

Idolatry, then, the leading characteristic of religious apostasy, was widely prevalent in the Roman Church at least as early as the sixth and seventh centuries [o]; and in the eighth the conscientious, though unsuccessful, opposition of the Eastern Emperors only served to confirm its uncontrolled dominion; while the corrupt decrees of the second Nicene Council [p] invested it with the high sanction of acknowledged authority. The whole train of superstitions and abuses now followed in rapid succession; monastic austerities, clerical celibacy, the systematic imposture of pretended miracles, the portentous delusions of Purgatory [q] and Transubstantiation, and the especial worship of the Virgin Mary [r]; in short, almost all the well known attributes

[n] Gen. iii. 6.

[o] " The use and even the worship of images was firmly " established before the end of the sixth century." *Gibbon, Decline and Fall*, vol. IX. p. 118.

[p] A. D. 787.

[q] " The doctrine of Purgatory was carried to a great " height in the *tenth* century." *Mosheim, Eccl. Hist.* vol. II. p. 417.

[r] " The worship of the Virgin Mary also, which had been " previously carried to a great degree of idolatry, received " further accessions in the tenth century. Her rosary and " crown may be traced to this age." *Ibid.* p. 429.

of Popery, attained their full developement
in the eleventh century; and even at this
early period had aroused the first display of
that strenuous opposition, which, afterwards
designated by the name of Protestantism, has
ever since resisted her pretensions[s].

Two glaring abuses were yet wanting to
complete the dreadful catalogue; the prohibition of Scripture, and the establishment of
the Inquisition[t]. They were adopted indeed
for the very purpose of maintaining her inveterate corruptions, and persevered in with a
skilfulness of policy and a remorseless energy
of purpose, which enabled her to ward off for
three full centuries, and eventually to render
incomplete, the triumph of the Reformation;—
though at the same time she effected this
through deeds of cruelty and slaughter, and
a reckless destruction of human life, which
cast into the shade even the blood-stained
records of Pagan persecution, realizing the
most revolting feature of her prophetic por-
trait—"drunken with the blood of the saints[u]."

[s] " A religious sect at Orleans, in 1017, and another in
" Flanders, in 1025, opposed Transubstantiation, the Invo-
" cation of Saints, and other Popish doctrines and practices.
" The first were burnt for their supposed heresy; the others
" were persuaded to recant." *Dupin, Histoire de l'Eglise en
abrégé*, III. 187, 188. Paris, 1726.

[t] These originated in the daring and skilful policy of Innocent III. at the beginning of the thirteenth century.

[u] Rev. xvii. 7.

In defiance, as it were, of these the plainest facts of history, the fatal Council of Trent is now declared to have made the Church of Rome what she is, and to have " given her a " new character, which has in a great mea- " sure disqualified us from passing an accu- " rate judgment upon her old one [x]." It has indeed, in one sense, given her a new and most awful character. Through an infatuation, bearing to human apprehension the fearful aspect of judicial blindness, it has pledged and committed the Papacy to continue, under the light of improved intelligence, every cor- ruption of faith and practice, which had marked her course through ages of darkness and superstition ; it has set the seal of immu- tability on the abominations of previous cen- turies, cutting her off even from the power of repentance, and from every apparent hope of escaping that dreadful doom which has been denounced on her persevering apostasy.

But are we required to infer from hence, that before the Reformation, though corrupt indeed and superstitious, she was compara- tively free from many of her grossest abuses? —that but for the unreasonable violence of the Reformers, her Communion might by possibi- lity have been maintained?—that consequent- ly these Reformers were the authors rather of

[x] British Critic for July 1836, p. 53.

evil than of good ?—Surely, however, little short
of this can be intended by that systematic advocacy of the Romish Church with which we
are now assailed ;—by the growing disposition
to palliate her errors, and even to commend
and admire and imitate a portion, at least, of
her system and practice. We are called upon
to regard her as " God's favoured instrument
" of good [y];" as " the chosen method in the
" Councils of Providence for keeping Christi-
" anity in reverence [z];" as " playing an im-
" portant part as the conservator of Christian-
" ity ;" as " our spiritual parent, over whose
" errors in her earlier days we should duti-
" fully mourn [a]." We are reminded, that " the
" vaunted antiquity, the universality, the una-
" nimity of their church, puts the Papists
" above the varying fashions of the world, and
" the religious novelties of the day [b]."

On the other hand, our understandings, as
well as our feelings, are outraged by insinua-
tions against " the *so called* Reformers [c]," and
the error of those who speak of the " blessed

[y] British Critic for July 1836, p. 79.

[z] Ibid. p. 80.

[a] Ibid. p. 82.

[b] Tracts for the Times, vol. I. No. 20. p. 3. See Appendix, Note G.

[c] " The glory of the English Church is, that it has taken
" the *Via Media,* as it has been called. It lies between the
" (so called) Reformers and the Romanists." *Ibid.* No. 38.
p. 6.

" Reformation [d]." We are even reproached for our " odious Protestantism [e];" for " regarding " the Papacy as a devastating phenomenon; " for fixing as well as we can the exact epoch " of its appearance, and for reckoning up the " years that have since elapsed, as though won- " dering that the continuance of such a pest " through so lengthened a period should have " been foredoomed in the Councils of Heaven [f]." Again, it is rashly—let us hope not insidiously —suggested, that we are " a *Reformed, not a* " *Protestant* Church [g];" and the eager desire is expressed to " *unprotestantise* [h]" us, at the very moment when the corrupt and debasing

[d] " I shall beg them to reproach me not with *Popery*, but " with *Protestantism*, and to be impartial enough to assail " not only me, but ' the blessed Reformation,' as they often " call it, using words they do not understand." *Ibid.* p. 8.

[e] " I must go about the country to look for the stray sheep " of the true fold; there are many about, I am sure; only " that odious Protestantism sticks in people's gizzard." *Froude's Remains*, vol. I. p. 322.

[f] British Critic for July 1836, p. 55.

[g] " The English Church, as such, is *not* Protestant, only " politically, that is, externally, or so far as it has been made " an establishment, and subjected to national and foreign " influences. It claims to be merely *Reformed*, not Protest- " ant, and it repudiates any fellowship with the mixed mul- " titude which crowd together, whether at home or abroad, " under a mere political banner." *Tracts for the Times*, vol. III. No. 71. p. 32.

[h] " I wish you could get to know something of S. and " W. and un——ise, un-Protestantise, un-Miltonise them." *Froude's Remains*, vol. I. p. 332.

system against which it is our wisdom and our piety to *protest*, is once more spreading its toils around us; when, so far from decrying and weakening the honest and Protestant, but somewhat dormant prepossessions of our countrymen, we should raise the warning voice, should " cry aloud and spare not[h]," lest they " be destroyed for lack of knowledge[i]."

The world, in its present condition, if we regard the forms of religion professed, and the insignificant proportion even of the *name* of Christianity; and the sweeping deductions which we must thence make for corruptions and heresies, superstitions and idolatries, and the various departures from the " truth as it is " in Jesus," affords to the eye of human reason a prospect rather of despair than of cheering hope, not merely for Catholic Communion, but even for the success of the Gospel itself. But He is faithful who has promised, that there shall at length be " one fold and one " Shepherd[k]." The good seed has been sown in the unprecedented dispersion of the Scriptures; let us wait in faith and hope for the predicted harvest. Above all, let us not, through impatient zeal, and the premature and vain expectation of realizing Catholic views in the midst of the surrounding desola-

[h] Isaiah lviii. 1.

[i] Hosea iv. 6.   See Appendix, Note H.

[k] John x. 16.

tion, incautiously entangle ourselves in those mysteries of iniquity, from which God's mercy has once granted us so signal a deliverance. If we desire to be hereafter *Catholic*, not merely in theory and in prospect, but in happy experience, let us be assured that we must be strictly *Protestant* now; that we must zealously cultivate Gospel truth in our own Communion, and dream neither of fellowship nor compromise with those subtle and encroaching adversaries, who would finally involve us in the awful destinies of Rome.

And now, in the impressive language of Ezra—so appropriately cited by an eminent Prelate of our Church[1], for a similar purpose, but with prospects far less imminently hazardous and threatening than our own—" seeing that thou, our God, hast punished us "less than our iniquities deserve, and hast "given us such deliverance as this; should "we again break thy commandments, and "join in affinity with the people of these abominations, wouldest not thou be angry with "us till thou hadst consumed us, so that there "should be no remnant nor escaping[m]?"

[1] Bishop Newton on the Prophecies; ad finem.
[m] Ezra ix. 13, 14.

D

APPENDIX.

Note A. p. 13.

"La France n'est pas la seule où se manifeste ce re-
"tour éclatant de notre siècle vers les doctrines et les
"institutions de l'Église catholique. Le mouvement
"que je signale est Européen, et c'est son étendue qui
"atteste sa profondeur. En Angleterre, les ouvrages
"du docteur John Lingard et de Cobbett ont préludé à
"la réaction catholique qui s'opère dans ce pays et
"excite si violemment la rage des torys. Je ne vou-
"drais pas m'en rapporter à mon propre jugement sur
"un sujet où il est si facile de prendre ses désirs et
"ses espérances pour des réalités, si je n'avais le té-
"moignage même d'un savant Anglais, M. le docteur
"Wiseman, qui a prêché à Londres, il y a deux ans, des
"conférences catholiques dont le succès n'a été égalé
"que par celles de M. l'abbé Lacordaire à Paris. M.
"Wiseman, recteur du collège des Anglais à Rome, a
"lu cette année, à l'académie catholique de cette ville,
"une longue et curieuse dissertation sur *l'Etat actuel du*
"*Protestantisme en Angleterre.* Les faits nombreux cités
"dans ce travail nous montrent chez les esprits les plus
"éclairés de la Grande-Bretagne, non seulement l'aban-
"don des préjugés les plus invétérés contre le catholi-
"cisme, contre la cour Romaine, mais un retour décidé
"vers les doctrines de l'Église. C'est surtout au sein de
"la célèbre université d'Oxford que se manifestent ces
"symptômes de réaction, et M. Wiseman cite pour
"preuve un recueil de dissertations publié par les pro-
"fesseurs de cette université, sous le titre de *Traités*
"*pour les temps présens.*"—*Introduction par M. Alexandre
*de Saint-Chéron, à l'Histoire de la Papauté par M. Léo-
pold Ranke.* p. 15, 16. Paris 1838.

" .L'université d'Oxford est célèbre par le savoir de
" ceux qui la composent, par leur attachement à l'église
" Anglicane, et par leur zèle pour son ancienne doctrine.
" Ils ont consigné leurs opinions dans une suite de dis-
" sertations intitulées *Traités pour les temps présens*, dont
" ils viennent de publier le troisième tome. Il est cu-
" rieux d'observer les aveux qu'ils rendent à la vérité.". .
.... " Il ne faut pas s'éton-
" ner que ces dissertations aient été dénoncées par beau-
" coup de protestans comme prouvant une défection
" totale des doctrines de la réforme, et un rapproche-
" ment trop manifeste de la croyance catholique."—
L'Ami de la Religion, Samedi, 13 *Janvier*, 1838.

Note B. p. 17.

" He (Tertullian) thus at last timidly, or rather reve-
" rently, advances to set forth God's last provision
" against the malice of Satan, repentance after Baptism.
" ' God providing against these his poisons, though the
" door of *full oblivion* (ignoscentiæ) is closed, and the
" bolt of Baptism fastened up, alloweth *somewhat* still to
" be open............Full confession (exomologesis) is the
" discipline of prostrating and humbling the whole man ;
" enjoining a conversation which may excite pity ; it
" enacts as to the very dress and sustenance—to lie on
" sackcloth and ashes : the body defiled, the mind cast
" down with grief : those things, in which he sinned,
" changed by a mournful treatment : for food and drink,
" bread only and water, for the sake of life, not of the
" belly : for the most part to nourish prayer by fasting :
" to groan ; to weep ; to moan day and night before the
" Lord their God ; to embrace the knees of the Presby-
" ters and of the friends of God ; to enjoin all the bre-
" thren to pray for them. All this is contained in ' full
" confession,' with the view to recommend their repent-
" ance ; to honour the Lord by trembling at their peril ;
" by pronouncing on the sinner, to discharge the office

" of the indignation of God ; and *by temporal affliction,—*
" I say not to baffle, but—*to blot out eternal torment.*
" When therefore it rolls them on the earth, it the ra-
" ther raises them : when it defiles, it cleanses them :
" accusing, it excuses them : condemning, it absolves
" them.   In as far as thou sparest not thyself, in so far
" will God, be assured, spare thee.'

" It is not of course the outward instances and ex-
" pressions of grief, of which Tertullian speaks, which
" one would contrast with our modern practice ; al-
" though most sincere penitents will probably have found
" it a great hinderance to effectual repentance, that they
" were obliged to bear about the load of their grief in
" their own bosoms; that they might not outwardly
" mourn ; that they must go through the daily routine
" of life without unburdening their souls by a public
" confession ; that they could not, without the evils of
" private confession, obtain the prayers of God's ser-
" vants ; that their outward, must needs be at variance
" with, thwarting, contradicting their inward, life."—
Tracts for the Times, vol. II. No. 67. p. 60, 61.

" ' Since,' says St. Hermas, ' God knew the thoughts
" of the heart, and the weakness of man, and the mani-
" fold wickedness of the Devil, whereby he devises mis-
" chief against the servants of God—therefore the mer-
" ciful Lord had mercy on the work of his hands ; and
" he assigned that repentance, and gave me power over
" that repentance. And, therefore, I say unto you, that,
" after that great and holy calling, (Baptism,) if any be
" tempted by the Devil and sin, he has *one* repentance.
" But if he sin again, and repent, it will not profit the
" man who doth such things, for hardly will he live to
" God.'.............. This passage of St. Hermas is the
" more remarkable, since he lays down the principle,
" upon which more than one repentance after Baptism
" would probably be very rare, if not altogether hope-
" less, coinciding with the *known teaching* of the Apostles,

" and with subsequent experience, although *limiting* very
" awfully what their *written teaching* has left undefined."
..................." ' As there is *one* Baptism,' says St. Am-
" brose, ' so also *one* repentance—one, I say, public re-
" pentance—for we ought to repent of our daily sins ;
" but this repentance is for lighter offences, that for
" heavier............*The world must be renounced.* Sleep
" itself must be less indulged than nature requires, must
" be interrupted with groans, must be sequestrated for
" prayer. *We must live so as to die to this life.* Man
" must deny himself, and be wholly changed.' " *Ibid.*
p. 67, 68, 69.

Note C. page 22.

" So then, none of the Protestant Churches doubt of
" the *real* (that is, true and not imaginary) presence of
" Christ's Body and Blood in the Sacrament ; and there
" appears no reason why any man should suspect their
" common confession, of either fraud or error, as though
" in this particular they had in the least departed from
" the Catholic faith."...............

" As for the opinion and belief of the German Pro-
" testants, it will be known chiefly by the Augustan Con-
" fession, presented to Charles the Fifth by the Princes
" of the Empire, and other great persons. For they
" teach..............' that the Body and Blood of Christ
" are truly present, and distributed to the Communi-
" cants in the Lord's Supper.' ....

" The Confession of Wittemberg, which in the year
" 1552 was propounded to the Council of Trent, is like
" unto this : for it teacheth that ' the true Body and
" Blood of Christ are given in the Holy Communion ;'
" and refutes those that say, ' that the Bread and Wine
" in the Sacrament are only signs of the absent Body
" and Blood of Christ.'............

" Bucerus, in the name of all the rest, (the divines
" of Basil and Strasbourg,) did freely answer.........
" ' that the true Body and Blood of Christ was truly

" presented, given, and received *together with* the visible
" signs of Bread and Wine'.........and did also main-
" tain this doctrine of the blessed Sacrament in pre-
" sence of the Landgrave of Hesse and Melancthon, con-
" fessing ' that *together with* the Sacrament we truly and
" substantially receive the Body of Christ.'............

" ' The Son of God (says Calvin) offers daily to us in
" the Holy Sacrament the same body which he once
" offered in sacrifice to his Father, that it may be our
" spiritual food.' .... He asserts as clearly as any
" one can, the true, *real*, and substantial presence and
" communication of the Body of Christ, &c." *Tracts for
the Times*, vol. I. No. 27. p. 3–9. (viz. *Bp. Cosin's History
of Transubstantiation*.)

.........." Berengarius was commanded presently with-
" out any delay to recant in that form prescribed.........
" by Cardinal Humbert; which was thus : 'I Berengarius,
" &c., assent to the Holy Roman and Apostolic See, and
" with my heart and mouth do profess that I hold that
" faith concerning the Sacrament of the Lord's Table,
" which our Lord and venerable Pope Nicholas, and this
" sacred Council, have determined and imposed upon
" me by their evangelic and apostolic authority ; to wit,
" that the Bread and Wine which are set on the altar,
" are not after the consecration only a sacrament, sign,
" and figure, but also the very Body and Blood of our
" Lord Jesus Christ ;' (*thus far it is well enough*, but what
" follows is too horrid, and is *disowned by the Papists
" themselves* ;) ' and that they' (the Body and Blood) ' are
" touched and broken with the hands of the Priests, and
" ground with the teeth of the faithful, not sacrament-
" ally only, but in truth and sensibly.' " *Ibid.* No. 28.
(viz. *Bp. Cosin continued*.)

It will be difficult to imagine that those who adopt
the views of Bishop Cosin fall much, if at all, short of
what has been commonly termed *Consubstantiation*. And
be it observed, that the more reasonable of the Papists

practically recede from the grossness of strict *Transub-stantiation.* For (as Mr. Perceval remarks) " the defi-
" nitions of the Council of Trent will upon examination
" be found to be so vague, so inconsistent, so self-con-
" tradictory, as to afford latitude for almost any expla-
" nation; and in point of practice, the most different
" opinions upon the point have been broached and openly
" maintained by different individuals in the Roman Com-
" munion. Thus while Harding the Jesuit contends
" that Christ was *twice immolated;* has *twice* shed his
" blood, once in the 'Eucharist, and once on the cross;
" and that the sacrifice of the Eucharist is a *reiteration* of
" that upon the cross;—while Le Quien maintains that
" the sacrifice of the Eucharist is a real sacrifice, and a
" *continuation* of that upon the cross; Cardinal Perron
" declares that the Christian sacrifice is a *figure or pat-*
" *tern* (figure ou exemplaire) of that upon the cross;
" Cassander, that Christ is there offered by *mystical re-*
" *presentation and commemoration.*" *The Roman Schism
illustrated, by the Hon. and Rev. A. P. Perceval*, p. 338.

Note D. p. 22.

" It is observable that the doctrine of the Fathers
" with regard to *Consecration* was much the same in
" relation to the waters of Baptism, as in relation to the
" elements in the Eucharist. They supposed a kind of
" descent of the *Holy Ghost*, to *sanctify* the waters in
" one, and the symbols in the other, to the uses intended;
" and they seem to have gone upon the general Scrip-
" tural principle, (besides particular texts relating to
" each Sacrament,) that the Holy Ghost is the immediate
" fountain of all Sanctification. I believe they were right
" in the main thing, only not always accurate in expres-
" sion. Had they said that the *Holy Ghost* came upon
" the *recipients*, in the *due use* of the Sacraments, they
" had spoken with greater exactness; and, perhaps, it
" was all that they really meant. They could not be
" aware of the disputes which might arise in after-

" times, nor think themselves obliged to a philosophical
" strictness of expression. It was all one for them to
" say, in a confuse general way, either that the Holy
" Ghost *sanctified the Receivers in the use of the outward*
" *symbols*, or that he *sanctified the symbols to their use;* for
" either expression seemed to amount to the same thing,
" though in strictness there is a considerable difference
" between them. What Mr. Hooker very judiciously
" says of the *real presence* of Christ in the Sacrament,
" appears to be equally applicable to the *presence* of the
" *Holy Spirit* in the same;"—" *It is not to be sought for*
" *in the Sacrament, but in the worthy Receiver of the*
" *Sacrament.*" *Waterland on the Eucharist,* p. 126, 127.
edit. 1737.

We need not therefore be surprised to find that those
who hold the doctrine of the *real presence,* without regard to this essential distinction, become dissatisfied
with the service of our Church, and betray an *approximation, at least,* to the superstitious views of Popery.—
Thus:

" I am more and more indignant at the Protestant
" doctrine on the subject of the Eucharist, and think
" that the principle on which it is founded is as proud,
" irreverent, and foolish, as that of any heresy, even
" Socinianism." *Froude's Remains,* vol. I. p. 391.

" By the bye, vide Bull's Works, vol. II. p. 225. ' we
" are not ignorant that the ancient Fathers generally
" teach that the bread and wine in the Eucharist, by or
" upon the consecration of them, do become and *are*
" *made* the Body and Blood of Christ.'" *Froude's Remains,*
vol. I. p. 363.

Note E. p. 25.

" Rome, stung by this rejection (viz. by our Thirty-
" Nine Articles) of doctrines in which the credit of her
" existing authorities was involved, adopted the bold—
" the unprecedented—step of formally incorporating
" these doctrines so completely with her religion, as to

" make the reception of them a necessary condition for
" participation in her communion. And this step it is
" which virtually separates us from that communion at
" the present hour. We commonly think and speak of
" our Reformers, as though they had separated them-
" selves from the Church of Rome, and put her to the
" ban. But such is not the fact; for aught that they
" have done, we could communicate with her *now*;—
" but we know, that should we attempt to do so, she
" would put forth this *list of novel dogmas of faith*, and
" call upon us either to subscribe it, or to depart from
" her altars." *British Critic, for July* 1836. p. 52.

" By incorporating, at Trent, her prevalent errors into
" the essence of her faith, Rome underwent, at that im-
" portant crisis, an absolute change of position." ......
" In such a position the Papacy has, as far as its own
" internal character has been concerned, from that period
" remained. Nor of that position, would we—durst we—
" become the apologists. Our quarrel with it, as it *now*
" is, is as deep as can be that of the most fiery champion
" among the ranks of protestantism." *Ibid.* p. 82.

Note F. p. 28.

If the Roman Church be really that predicted Apostasy, which the most approved interpreters of Prophecy unanimously maintain, we may rest assured, that
every encouragement afforded to a system thus offensive
in the sight of Heaven, whether by the grant of political
influence, or by any general disposition to relapse into
her errors, or even to relax from that strenuous resist-
ance to her power and principles, which was established at the Reformation, is a national *sin*, for which
the severest national chastisement may be reasonably anti-
cipated. This was precisely the view taken by the late
excellent Bishop Van Mildert, when, in his place in the
House of Lords, he joined in the ineffectual opposition
to what was called " Catholic emancipation."

" Convinced, too," said he, " as I am, (and that upon
" no light or superficial grounds, but after many years of
" studious consideration and inquiry,) that the religion
" of Popery is distinctly and awfully pointed out in
" Scripture, as the one great apostasy from the truth,
" the declared object of Divine displeasure, I feel that
" I should not be discharging the duty I owe to a
" far higher tribunal than your Lordships', if I as-
" sented to any thing which I believed to have a ten-
" dency to strengthen or uphold such a corrupt and
" erroneous system. . . . . . I dare not be instrumental
" in uniting Popery with Protestantism, nor in destroy-
" ing or weakening the distinction between idolatrous
" superstition, and the pure worship of God in spirit and
" in truth." *Memoir of Bishop Van Mildert, prefixed to
his Sermons and Charges*, p. 103.

Note G. p. 34.

The growing disposition to advocate, as far as may
be, the cause of Popery, to excuse her errors, to admire,
and even in some points to adopt, her principles and
practice, is seen in numerous instances. A few specimens are the following :—

" Those who have not leisure or inclination to investi-
" gate the subject, find it convenient to view the doctrines
" of Transubstantiation, Purgatory, Image-worship, and
" the like, as though incorporated with each other, and
" with the Papal dominion in an essential unity . . . .
" Whereas the fact is, that for the origin of most of
" these abuses the Pontiffs are not in any degree re-
" sponsible." *British Critic for July* 1836. p. 73.

" Although the details of the early ritual varied in
" importance, and corrupt additions were made in the
" middle ages, yet as a whole the Catholic ritual was a
" precious possession ; and if we who have escaped from
" Popery, have lost not only the possession, but the

" sense of its value, it is a serious question whether we
" are not like men who recover from some grievous
" illness with the loss or injury of their sight or hear-
" ing;—whether we are not like the Jews returned from
" captivity, who could never find the Rod of Aaron or
" the Ark of the Covenant." *Tracts for the Times*, vol. I.
No. 34.

We have afterwards specimens of services from the
Roman Breviary, and even *a design for a service for
March* 21st, *the day of Bishop Ken's death*, as though he
were selected as a candidate for a place in the Romish
Calendar. The addresses to the Virgin are explained
to be in general comparatively modern; but for one or
two confessedly ancient we find this singular defence.—
" As to the Confession at Prime and Compline, in which
" is introduced the name of the blessed Virgin and
" other Saints, this practice stands on a different ground.
" It is not a simple gratuitous Invocation made to them,
" but it is an address to Almighty God *in his Heavenly
" Court*, as surrounded by his Saints and Angels, an-
" swering to St. Paul's charge to Timothy, ' before God
" and the Lord Jesus Christ, and the elect Angels,' and
" to Daniel and St. John's address to the Angels who
" were sent to them. The same may even be said of the
" Invocation ' Holy Mary and all Saints, &c.' in the
" Prime Service, which Gavanti describes as being of
" very great antiquity." The Confession however stands
thus:

" I confess before God Almighty, before the blessed
" Mary, Ever-Virgin, the blessed Michael Archangel,
" the blessed John Baptist, the Holy Apostles Peter
" and Paul, before All Saints, and you, my brethren,
" that I have sinned, &c. &c. Therefore, *I beseech thee,*
" blessed Mary, Ever-Virgin, the blessed Michael Arch-
" angel, &c. &c. *to pray the Lord our God for me.*"
Tracts for the Times, vol. III. No. 75. p. 10 and 61.

" Why is the opinion of the English Clergy, since the
" enactment of the Prayer Book, entitled to be called
" the teaching of the Church, more than that of the
" Clergy of the sixteen previous centuries? or, again,
" than the Clergy of France, Italy, Spain, Russia, &c. &c.?
" I can see no other claim which the Prayer Book has
" on a layman's deference, as the teaching of the Church,
" which the Breviary and Missal have not in a far greater
" degree."—*Froude's Remains*, vol. I. p. 402.

" I am sure the Daily Service is a great point ; so is
" kneeling with your back to the people, which, by the
" bye, seems to be striking all apostolicals at once : I
" see there are letters on it in the British Magazine."—
Ibid. p. 390.

" You will be shocked at my avowal that I am every
" day becoming a less and less loyal son of the Reform-
" ation. It appears to me plain that in all matters that
" seem to us indifferent, or even doubtful, we should
" *conform our practices* to those of the Church which has
" preserved its *traditionary* practices unbroken. We
" cannot know about any seemingly indifferent practice
" of the Church of Rome, that it is not a developement
" of the apostolic ἦθος; and it is to no purpose to say
" that we can find no proof of it in the writings of the
" six first centuries ; they must find a *dis*-proof, if they
" would do any thing." *Ibid.* p. 336.

" I forgot to say that ——— has derived great relief
" from the distinction between *catholic verities* and *theo-*
" *logical opinions,* as affecting the case of us with the
" evangelicals, and thinks we can fraternize with them
" without liberalism. Also he admits that, if the Roman
" Catholics would revoke their anathemas, *we might*
" *reckon all the points of difference as theological opinions.*
" *This τόπος is a good one."* *Ibid.* p. 329.

" I see Hammond takes that view of the *infallibility*
" of the Church, which P. says was the old one. *We*

" *must revive it.* Surely the promise, ' I am with you " always,' means something." *Ibid.* p. 322.

" It has lately come into my head, that the present " state of things in England makes an opening for re- " viving the *monastic system.* I think of putting the " view forward under the title of ' Project for reviving " Religion in great Towns.'" *Ibid.*

" I touched just now on the subject of the Religious " Institutions of the middle ages. These are impera- " tively called for to stop the progress of dissent : indeed, " I conceive you necessarily must have dissent or *mo-* " *nachism* in a Christian Country ; so make your choice. " .... Heathens and quasi heathens (such as the " miserable rabble of a large town) were not converted " in the beginning of the gospel, or now, as it would " appear, by the sight of domestic virtues or domestic " comforts in a missionary." *British Magazine for April* 1836. p. 366—368.

" Since they (the early Church) knew not of our chill " separation between those *who being dead* in Christ, live " to Christ and with Christ, and those *who are yet in the* " *flesh,* they felt assured that this sacrifice offered by the " Church on earth, for the whole Church, conveyed to " that portion of the Church, which *had passed into the* " *unseen world, such benefits* of Christ's death as (their " conflicts over and they at rest) were still applicable to " them,......... Why should we take upon ourselves to " say that they who are His members as well as we, " have no interest in this, which is offered as a memo- " rial for all ? or why should men think it an unhappi- " ness or imperfection that they should *obtain additional* " *joys and satisfactions thereby ?—Tracts for the Times,* vol. IV. No. 81. p. 6, 7.

" The receiving of which Sacrament or participating " of which Sacrifice exhibited to us, we say is profitable " only to them that receive it and participate of it ; but " the *prayers* that we add thereunto, in presenting the

" death and merits of our Saviour to God, are not only
" beneficial to them that are present, but to them that
" are absent also, *to the dead and the living both*, to all
" true members of the Catholic Church of Christ." (Extract from Bishop Cosin.)—*Ibid*. p. 136.

There appears a reluctance to admit *fully* the *Idolatry* of the Church of Rome. Thus :—

" I think people are injudicious who talk against the
" Roman Catholics for worshipping Saints and honour-
" ing the Virgin and images, &c.;—these things *may*
" *perhaps be idolatrous*—I cannot make up my mind
" about it." *Froude's Remains*, vol. I. p. 294.

" The direct invocation of saints is a *dangerous* prac-
" tice, as *tending to give*, often actually giving, to crea-
" tures the honour and reliance due to the Creator alone."
Tracts for the Times, vol. I. No. 38. p. 12.

Note H. page 36.

.... " I am not speaking of those who would ad-
" mit they were Puritans ; but of that *arrogant Pro-*
" *testant spirit* (so called) of the day, in and out of the
" Church, (if it is possible to say what is in and what is
" out,) which thinks it takes bold and large views, and
" would fain ride over the superstitions and formalities,
" which it thinks it sees in those who (I maintain) hold
" to the old Catholic faith." *Tracts for the Times*, vol. I.
No. 41. p. 12.

" The wiseacres are all agog about our being Papists.
" P. called us ' the Papal Protestant Church ;'—in which
" he proved a double ignorance, as we are Catholics with-
" out the Popery, and Church-of-England men *without*
" *the Protestantism*." *Froude's Remains*, vol. I. p. 404.

" I do believe that he (R——) hates the *meagreness of*
" *Protestantism* as much as either of us." *Ibid*. p. 425.

This perpetual attempt to cry down and depreciate
the principles of Protestantism, and to connect its very
name with all that is odious and disreputable, cannot be

too strongly reprobated. Popery having once more become the assailant, *Protestantism* is the very *bond of union* for our Church and nation, the *watchword* for our defence; and the dissemination of such religious views, as those which I have endeavoured to expose, has become doubly dangerous.

Unaccountable is the indiscretion, and heavy the responsibility of those, who have sent forth the offensive publication, from which the most startling and extravagant of my extracts have been taken. With many persons indeed its very extravagance will be a sufficient antidote to the poison which it contains. But who shall answer for its effect on the public mind in these days of unsettled principles and religious disunion, should it, by some unhappy chance, obtain extensive circulation?

If any considerable party have concurred with the editors in the hearty approval of its sentiments and views, then is there a far more formidable *conspiracy*[a] against our principles and our welfare, than most of us have hitherto dreamed of. If, on the other hand, the editors themselves (as is partially intimated[b]) do not wholly coincide in every opinion which it expresses, who is to separate the *tares* from the *wheat?* It becomes a wanton *experiment* on popular weakness and credulity— a wilful *tampering* with the faith and happiness of thousands.

[a] " R. thinks biography the best means of infusing principles against " the reader's will." *Froude's Remains*, vol. I. p. 321.

Preface, p. xxii.